This Country Belongs to:

_____

ALASKA

HAWAII

CONTIGUOUS FORTY-EIGHT STATES

TERRITORIES

For Tom, Jake, and Ella —KM

To Henry, Amanda, and Alexis—
who aren't allowed to be president,
but you'd be lucky to have them —AR

THE *Next* PRESIDENT

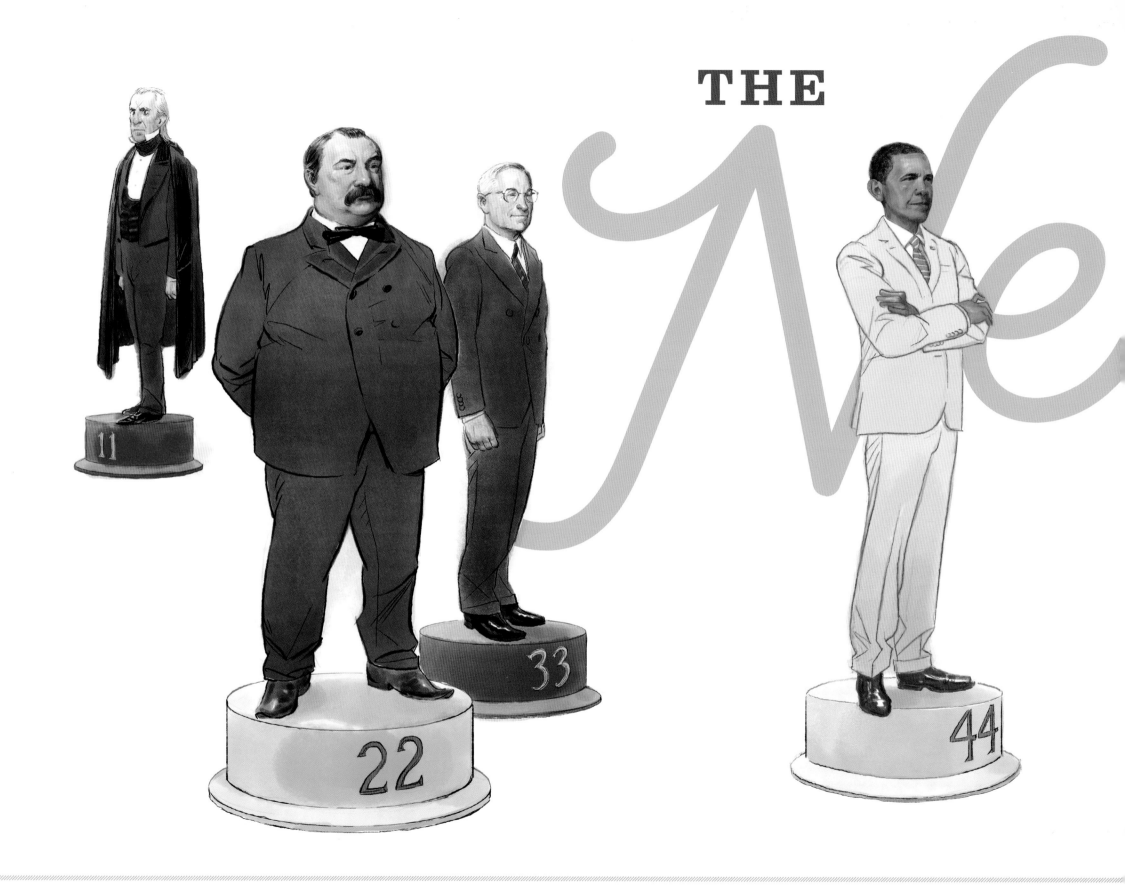

★ ★ ★ ★ ★ ★ ★ ★ ★ ★ ★ ★ ★ ★ ★ ★ ★ ★ ★

Next PRESIDENT

The Unexpected Beginnings and Unwritten Future of America's Presidents

Kate Messner

★

Adam Rex

chronicle books · san francisco

Quick:

NAME THE PRESIDENT *of the* UNITED STATES.

★ ★ ★ ★ ★

No matter when you read this book, there's only one right answer to that question, because America only has one president at a time.

But no matter who holds the job right now, the presidents of tomorrow are always out there somewhere.

Some already know they'd like to run the country one day. Some are learning how government works as members of Congress or representatives in state, local, or student government.

40

And some don't have a clue yet that one day, they'll be president.

When George Washington became the first president of the United States, there were **NINE** future presidents already alive in America. Four of them were working alongside Washington in the nation's new capital.

President 2, John Adams, was Washington's vice president. Adams was known for having a short temper and getting into arguments. He was the only one of the first five presidents who didn't enslave people.

President 3, Thomas Jefferson, served as secretary of state. In 1776, he had written the Declaration of Independence, which includes the words "all men are created equal"—even though Jefferson enslaved hundreds of people on his Virginia plantation.

President 4, James Madison, had grown up on a plantation in Virginia, and now represented that state in the nation's new Congress. Madison wasn't always easy to hear with his quiet voice, and he ended up being America's smallest president. Madison was 5 feet, 4 inches tall and only weighed about 100 pounds.

President 5, James Monroe, had run for Congress, too, but he'd lost to Madison. Monroe would be elected to the Senate the following year. Like many other future presidents, he'd intended to study law in college—but he dropped out to join the army.

1789.

At the time of Washington's inauguration, Presidents 6 and 7 were both practicing law . . .

President 7, Andrew Jackson, was living in a boardinghouse in Nashville. Jackson was the son of Irish immigrants. His father had died before he was born, and he'd grown up with a reputation as an outsider with a furious temper.

President 6, John Quincy Adams, was about to open his own legal practice in Boston. As a boy, he'd traveled overseas with his father to ask France for help during the Revolutionary War.

. . . while Presidents 8, 9, and 12 were all kids.
(Presidents 10 and 11 hadn't been born yet.)

President 8, Martin Van Buren, was seven years old, helping with chores on his parents' farm in Kinderhook, NY.

President 9, William Henry Harrison, was 16 years old and studying medicine.

President 12, four-year-old Zachary Taylor, was living with his two older brothers on the Kentucky farmland his father had been given for serving in the Revolutionary War.

After 19 years in law and politics, and another 23 years before he'd be president, **Andrew Jackson** was running a Tennessee cotton plantation. He'd been in fights and duels before, but this time, it was more serious. It all started when a man named Charles Dickinson accused Jackson of cheating on a horse bet and insulted Jackson's wife. Dickinson fired the first shot and hit Jackson close to his heart. But before Jackson fell, he fired back, killing Dickinson. The bullet that hit Jackson was too close to his heart for doctors to remove, and Jackson would carry it with him all the way to the White House in 1829.

33 years before he would be president, **Abraham Lincoln** *was on his way to New Orleans, working on a Mississippi riverboat full of farm produce. Lincoln cooked, navigated, and did whatever else was needed to help out.*

1841.

When William Henry Harrison became President 9, there were FOURTEEN future presidents alive. Most of them were already involved in politics somehow.

President 10, John Tyler, had worked as a lawyer, congressman, and senator before he was elected to be Harrison's vice president. Some historians have called Tyler "the accidental president" because he had to take over when Harrison died of pneumonia just 31 days into his term.

President 23, Little Benjamin Harrison, who was seven years old, wasn't *actually* there for the inauguration but probably wished he could have seen that moment. He must have been proud when his grandpa, William Henry Harrison, took the oath of office.

President 11, James K. Polk, had a setback that year. He had been governor of Tennessee, but didn't get reelected. He lost to a 6-foot-2, 125-pound man with the nickname "Lean Jimmy Jones."

Polk didn't give up on politics, though. He started talking with people about his desire to be nominated for vice president.

And little Zachary Taylor, President 12, was grown up and serving in the military now.

Presidents 13, 14, 15, 16, and 17 were all serving in government then.

1841

President 13, Millard Fillmore, who'd grown up as a quiet bookworm in Central New York, was in Congress.

President 14, Franklin Pierce, had been serving as a senator, but left Washington in 1841 to go home to New Hampshire at his wife's request.

President 15, James Buchanan, was in the Senate in 1841. Sixteen years later, he would become the only president who never got married.

President 16, Abraham Lincoln, was serving in the Illinois legislature then. He'd done lots of other jobs before that. As a young man, Lincoln built things, sold groceries, did farm chores, and rowed a ferry boat.

And **President 17,** Andrew Johnson, was elected to the state senate in Tennessee. He'd moved there with a cart and pony way back in 1825, after he ran away from the tailor to whom he'd been apprenticed.

1841.

Presidents 18 and 19 were both in college in 1841.

President 18, Ulysses S. Grant, was attending the United States Military Academy at West Point, preparing for his time in the armed forces.

President 19, Rutherford B. Hayes, was studying at Kenyon College, preparing for a career in law. He had a reputation as a pretty good cook, even though cooking in student rooms was against the rules.

Presidents 20, 21, and 22, were all busy growing up.

President 20, James Garfield, was working on an Ohio farm with his brothers and his mom.

President 21, Chester A. Arthur, was in school, but he moved around a lot with his father, a preacher who traveled from town to town.

President 22, and later, **President 24,** Grover Cleveland, also had a dad who was a preacher. His family traveled from church to church, too. Whenever he could, he snuck away to fish.

For **President 23,** see page 14.

Snapshot:

After serving in the Illinois General Assembly and losing a race for U.S. Senate, **ABRAHAM LINCOLN** finally made it to the White House . . . and brought along two goats, Nanny and Nanko. Nanny used to get in trouble for eating blossoms out of the flowerbeds.

Lincoln wasn't the only president with a penchant for pets. **WARREN HARDING** had an Airedale named Laddie Boy, who used to attend cabinet meetings with the president.

When **CALVIN COOLIDGE** was in the White House, Mrs. Coolidge had a raccoon named Rebecca that she took for walks on a leash. And then there was William Johnson Hippopotamus (nicknamed Billy), a pygmy hippo the president received as a gift in 1927. (Billy ended up spending most of his life at the National Zoo.)

THEODORE ROOSEVELT'S *White House visitors might have met Bill the lizard, Maude the pig, Josiah the badger, Baron Spreckle the hen, or Peter the rabbit. The Roosevelts also had a hyena, a barn owl, some ducks in the fountain, an Icelandic pony named Algonquin, a small bear named Jonathan Edwards, and a handful of snakes. One of the snakes belonged to First Daughter Alice, who said she named it Emily Spinach because it was green and as thin as her Aunt Emily.*

Meanwhile, **THOMAS JEFFERSON** *and* **WILLIAM McKINLEY** *were partial to birds. Jefferson had a mockingbird named Dick, who perched on his shoulder sometimes while he worked. And McKinley had a parrot named Washington Post, who could supposedly whistle the song "Yankee Doodle."*

1897.

When **President 25,** William McKinley, moved into the White House with his Vice President, Garret Hobart, there were **NINE** future presidents alive.

President 26, Theodore Roosevelt, was serving as Assistant Secretary of the Navy. It might not have seemed very exciting after his wild years as a cattle rancher in the Badlands of South Dakota. But before long, Roosevelt would get a bigger job. He'd become vice president after the death of Garret Hobart.

President 27, William Howard Taft, was serving as a judge and teaching at the University of Cincinnati Law School. Taft was a big man who had a reputation as a fighter and a wrestler when he was growing up.

Other future presidents were busy with different jobs.

President 28, Woodrow Wilson, was teaching at Princeton University and liked to ride his bike around campus.

President 29, Warren G. Harding, was running the *Marion Star,* an Ohio newspaper he'd purchased with two friends.

President 30, Calvin Coolidge, was working as a lawyer in Northampton, Massachusetts. He'd learned all about hard work helping out in his father's general store when he was a kid. He'd worn his hair on the long side in college, but he had it cut shorter when he took the job in law and realized what serious work he would be doing.

President 31, Herbert Hoover, had studied engineering in college, and was managing a gold-mining operation in Australia.

1897.

Presidents 32, 33, and 34 were kids then.

President 32, Franklin Delano Roosevelt, was 15 and loved sailing when his family vacationed in Maine. Roosevelt was a collector, too. He kept detailed notebooks about his postage stamp, bird nest, and egg collections.

President 33, Harry Truman, who was turning thirteen that year, played piano and loved to read, especially biographies. Later on, before he became president, he would work as a timekeeper for a railroad gang and spend time farming cows and pigs.

President 34, seven-year-old Dwight D. Eisenhower, was helping out in the family garden with his brothers. The boys also worked at their father's creamery after school. When he had free time, Dwight liked playing baseball and football.

THEODORE ROOSEVELT *wins the prize for President Who Had the Most Adventures on his Way to the White House. After he finished law school, he took off for Europe and climbed the Matterhorn in the Alps. He moved out West for a while, bought a ranch in South Dakota, and spent his time riding, roping, and hunting.*

Even after Roosevelt became Vice President in 1901, he snuck off to explore. He was climbing Mount Marcy, the tallest peak in the Adirondacks, when a messenger arrived to tell him President William McKinley had taken a turn for the worse after being shot by an assassin in Buffalo. Roosevelt left for Buffalo the next day, but McKinley died before he got there. Roosevelt was sworn in as president before he could even unpack his bags. At 42, he became the youngest president to take office.

1961.

But it was **President 35,** John F. Kennedy, who was the youngest to be *elected to* the job. Kennedy was 43 years old when he took the oath of office. The next **TEN** presidents were alive then, too, scattered all across the country.

President 36, Lyndon Baines Johnson, was serving as JFK's vice president. That was a fancier job than others he'd held. As a kid, Johnson had shined shoes and picked cotton. After high school, he'd moved out to California to pick oranges and wash dishes to earn money for college.

President 37, Richard Nixon, had served as vice president under Dwight D. Eisenhower and hoped to be president next.

But he lost the 1960 election to Kennedy, so he left the White House and moved back to California. Many people think our nation's first televised debates had a big role in Nixon's defeat. TV was new then.

Nixon didn't practice as much as Kennedy did, and he also refused to use professional makeup, even though he'd been in the hospital recently. After the first debate, his mom called him on the phone to ask if he was feeling all right.

I'm *FINE,* Mom.

1961.

President 38, Gerald Ford, was serving in Congress. He'd come a long way from his awkward teenage years when he bought his first car, a $75 Ford coupe with a rumble seat . . . and promptly set it on fire by covering the hood with blankets on a winter night while the engine was still hot.

President 39, Jimmy Carter, was running a peanut farm in Georgia and serving on his local school board.

President 40, Ronald Reagan, was working as a TV host. Before becoming president, he had also announced play-by-play sports on the radio, acted in movies, and served as Governor of California.

President 41, George H. W. Bush, wouldn't lead the nation for another 28 years, but in 1961 he was president of an oil exploration company called Zapata Off-Shore.

1961.

And Presidents 42, 43, 44, and 45 were all kids.

President 42, Bill Clinton, was 15 years old and going to school in Arkansas, where he loved debate and playing tenor saxophone. In 1963, he would be chosen as a delegate to Boys Nation, where he'd meet President Kennedy and shake his hand.

President 43, George W. Bush (41's son!) was 15 in 1961, and attending prep school in Massachusetts. By senior year, he'd signed up for the cheerleading squad!

And **President 45,** Donald Trump, was a teenager then. He was attending New York Military Academy, where his father had hoped he'd learn some discipline.

President 44, Barack Obama, was born that year, the son of an American woman and a Kenyan man who'd met at the University of Hawaii. Their little boy would grow up to be the first African American president of the United States.

And where is the next president now? It's exciting to think about, isn't it?

But all those things have happened, because America is always changing. And it is changing now. When voters choose the next president, they won't look to the past, but to the future—and the ever-hopeful vision of what America *could* be.

The truth is America's earliest presidents weren't all that different from one another. Most were wealthy, white, Protestant men who might have been surprised if they'd been around to see a Catholic or an African American man elected president . . . or a woman nominated by a major party for the highest office in the land.

So where is the next president?

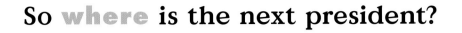

At least TEN

of our future presidents are probably alive today. If we go by the odds, three of them are likely serving in government somewhere already. One is in college or in the military. Three probably have other jobs—perhaps practicing law, building things, teaching, running a business. And at least three of our future presidents are kids.

What are they doing right now?

listening, LEARNING, and getting ready to LEAD.

Presidential **BIRTHPLACES**

America's presidency goes all the way back to 1789, when there were only twelve states in the union, so it makes sense that the oldest states have produced the most presidents. Virginia leads the list as the birthplace of eight presidents. Ohio comes in second, with seven, while New York produced five presidents.

Four presidents were born in Massachusetts, while North Carolina, Texas, and Vermont each produced two. South Carolina, New Hampshire, Pennsylvania, Kentucky, New Jersey, Iowa, Missouri, California, Nebraska, Georgia, Illinois, Arkansas, Connecticut, and Hawaii have each sent one president to Washington.

So far, America hasn't had any presidents who were born in Alabama, Alaska, Arizona, Colorado, Delaware, Florida, Idaho, Indiana, Kansas, Louisiana, Maine, Maryland, Michigan, Minnesota, Mississippi, Montana, Nevada, New Mexico, North Dakota, Oklahoma, Oregon, Rhode Island, South Dakota, Tennessee, Utah, Washington, West Virginia, Wisconsin, or Wyoming.

(But maybe YOU *will be the first!)*

PRESIDENTIAL REQUIREMENTS

All of America's presidents so far have been men—most of them white men. But that has to do with history, power, and privilege rather than the actual rules about who can be president.

The requirements to be president of the United States are explained clearly in the Constitution. None of them have to do with your gender, whether or not you have a disability, the color of your skin, where your ancestors are from, what you believe, or who you love:

"No Person except a natural born Citizen, or a Citizen of the United States, at the time of the Adoption of this Constitution, shall be eligible to the Office of President; neither shall any person be eligible to that Office who shall not have attained to the Age of thirty five Years, and been fourteen Years a Resident within the United States."

That means that in order to be president of the United States, a person has to:

- **Have been a citizen since birth**
- **Be at least 35 years old**
- **Have lived in the United States at least 14 years**

THE CHANGING FACE OF AMERICA'S PRESIDENCY

In 2009, Barack Obama took his oath of office as America's first African American president. He was re-elected to a second term in 2012. In 2016, Hillary Clinton became the first woman to be nominated for president by a major political party. She lost the election to Donald Trump. In the following midterm elections, more than a hundred women were elected to Congress, the greatest number ever. Many of them were inspired by Hillary Clinton's near victory!

A PRESIDENTIAL BOOKSHELF: SUGGESTIONS FOR FURTHER READING

Kid Presidents: True Tales of Childhood from America's Presidents. David Stabler. Illustrated by Doogie Horner. Quirk Books, 2014.

Lives of the Presidents: Fame, Same (and What the Neighbors Thought). Kathleen Krull. Illustrated by Kathryn Hewitt. HMH Books, 2011.

The New Big Book of U.S. Presidents. Todd David and Marc Frey. Running Press Kids, 2017.

So You Want to Be President? Judith St. George. Illustrated by David Small. Philomel Books, 2000.

Weird But True Know-It-All: U.S. Presidents. Brianna DuMont. National Geographic, 2017.

BIBLIOGRAPHY:

Barnard, Harry. *Rutherford B. Hayes and His America.* Indianapolis: The Bobbs-Merrill Company, 1954.

Barre, W.L. *Life and Public Services of Millard Fillmore.* New York: Burt Franklin, 1971.

Bausum, Ann. *Our Country's Presidents: A Complete Encyclopedia of the U.S. Presidency.* Washington, D.C.: National Geographic, 2017.

Berg, A. Scott. *Wilson.* New York: G.P. Putnam's Sons, 2013.

Borneman, Walter R. *Polk: The Man Who Transformed the Presidency and America.* New York: Random House, 2008.

Boyd, Bentley. "Reconstructing Rutherford B. Hayes." Kenyon College Bulletin. Volume 40.2
     Winter 2018. bulletin.kenyon.edu/feature/reconstructing-rutherford-b-hayes/

Brands, H.W. *Andrew Jackson: His Life and Times.* New York: Doubleday, 2005.

Brinkley, Douglas. *The Wilderness Warrior: Theodore Roosevelt and the Crusade for America.* New York: HarperCollins, 2009.

Chernow, Ron. *Washington: A Life.* New York: Penguin Press, 2010.

Clinton, Bill. *My Life.* New York: Alfred A. Knopf, 2004.

Crapol, Edward P. *John Tyler: The Accidental President.* Chapel Hill: University of North Carolina Press, 2006.

Cresson, W.P. *James Monroe.* Chapel Hill: University of North Carolina Press, 1946.

C-Span. American Presidents: Life Portraits. Accessed 1/25/18. Online:
     www.c-span.org/series/?presidents

Fausold, Martin L. *The Presidency of Herbert C. Hoover.* Lawrence, KS: University Press of Kansas, 1985.

Ferrell, Robert H. *The Presidency of Calvin Coolidge.* Lawrence, KS: University of Kansas Press, 1998.

Ford, Gerald. *A Time to Heal: The Autobiography of Gerald R. Ford.* New York: Harper & Row, 1979.

Ketchum, Ralph. *James Madison: A Biography.* Charlottesville, VA: University of Virginia Press, 1990.

Kohn, Edward P. *Heir to the Empire City: New York and the Making of Theodore Roosevelt.* New York: Basic Books, 2013.

McCoy, Donald R. *Calvin Coolidge: The Quiet President.* New York: The MacMillan Company, 1967.

McCullough, David. *Mornings on Horseback.* New York: Simon & Schuster, 1981.

Meacham, Jon. *American Lion: Andrew Jackson in the White House.* New York: Random House, 2008.

Meacham, Jon. *Destiny and Power: The American Odyssey of George Herbert Walker Bush.* New York: Random House, 2015.

Meacham, Jon. *Thomas Jefferson: The Art of Power.* New York: Random House, 2012.

Miller, Richard Lawrence. *Truman: The Rise to Power.* New York: McGraw-Hill Book Company, 1986.

Morgan, George. *The Life of James Monroe.* New York: AMS Press, 1969.

Morris, Edmund. *Theodore Rex.* New York: Random House, 2001.

Morris, Roger. *Richard Milhous Nixon: The Rise of an American Politician.* New York: Henry Holt, 1990.

Russell, Francis. *The Shadow of Blooming Grove: Warren Harding in His Times.* New York: McGraw-Hill Book Company, 1968.

Sievers, Harry J. *Benjamin Harrison: Hoosier Warrior.* New York: University Publishers Incorporated, 1952.

Unger, Harlow Giles. *John Quincy Adams.* Boston, MA: Da Capo Press, 2012.

Walworth, Arthur. *Woodrow Wilson, American Prophet.* New York: Longmans, Green, and Co., 1958.

Wilentz, Sean. *Andrew Jackson.* New York: Henry Holt & Company, 2005.

Text copyright © 2020 by Kate Messner.
Illustrations copyright © 2020 by Adam Rex.

Library of Congress Cataloging-in-Publication Data:
Names: Messner, Kate, author. | Rex, Adam, illustrator.
Title: The next president : the unexpected beginnings and unwritten future of America's presidents / by Kate Messner ; illustrated by Adam Rex.
Description: San Francisco, California : Chronicle Kids, Chronicle Books, 2020. | Audience: Grades 4-6. | Audience: Ages 8-12.

Identifiers: LCCN 2018052489 | ISBN 9781452174884 (alk. paper)

Subjects: LCSH: Presidents—United States—Biography—Juvenile literature.
Classification: LCC E176.8 .M47 2020 | DDC 973.09/9—dc23 LC record available at https://lccn.loc.gov/2018052489

Manufactured in China.

MIX
Paper from
responsible sources
FSC™ C104723

Design by Woody Harrington.
Typeset in Sentinel, Futura, Value Serif, and Garris.
The illustrations in this book were rendered digitally.

10 9 8 7 6 5 4 3 2 1

Chronicle Books LLC
680 Second Street
San Francisco, California 94107

Chronicle Books—we see things differently.
Become part of our community at www.chroniclekids.com.